To The Ronstadts

With gratitude for your hospitality

Best wishes

Michael Hough

March 2001

sydney AUSTRALIA

Photography by Darren Hopton

Little Hills Press

Little Hills Press Pty Ltd
Sydney, Australia
email: info@littlehills.com
http://www.littlehills.com

Photographs by Darren Hopton
Design work by Artitude
Editorial Team: Mark Truman, Chris Baker
Printed in Korea

Darren Hopton is a freelance photographer based in Sydney. He dedicates his work on this book to the memory of *Natasha Thomas* and *Flynn Evison*.
darrenhopton@hotmail.com

contents

Sydney Opera House
Commenced in 1957 and completed in 1973, this extraordinary building was designed by Jan Utzon and encapsulates the concept of architecture mimicking its environment. The white sails give the vague impression that the building is a cluster of vessels on the waters of Port Jackson. Now the symbol of Sydney, it has been elevated onto the world's list of premier attractions.

'he Harbour Brige & Opera House from North Sydney

)ne of the world's greatest marine backdrops, Sydney's superb icons are caught here ·mid the bustle of daytime activity, as people await a ferry on Luna Park Wharf, and passing yachts and small cruisers carve their white trails across the harbour.

the harbour and its outreaches

The Harbour from Sydney Tower
From the observation deck of Sydney Tower, this lofty view takes in the eastern edge of the CBD, sweeps over the Domain towards Mrs Macquarie's Chair and Garden Island, spreads across the water to exclusive Mosman real estate and fades into the North Shore suburbs. The tip of South Head occupies the distant right.

aturday Regatta, Rose Bay

ıchts berthed on the harbour foreshores take to the sea to compete in their aturday regatta. Shown here on a clear summer morning, with conditions ideal for recreational navigation, these vessels plot a course off Rose Bay, bounded by Clark Island in the foreground and Shark Island on the northern side.

Yachts moored at the Cruising Yacht Club, Rushcutters Bay

The best way to enjoy the spectacular scenery of Sydney Harbour is by drifting luxuriously in its centre. A sailing craft is almost a necessity for those who can afford one, and on weekends the water's surface is laced with tranquil patterns of whitewash. For the rest of the week, while corporate owners are in the city earning the money needed pay for them, these yachts bob softly at the marina, their many masts forming an impressive sight against the skyscape.

Pittwater

The beauty of Sydney is sourced at its harbour. Coastal formations and colours comprise a landscape that is sometimes reminiscent of tropical locations. Myriads of hidden inlets, arcing bays and threading tributaries ensure that one is never far from the water. Here, pictured on the right, a family picnics in seclusion at Pittwater on Sydney's northern peninsula. Shown on the left, this stretch of fertile land and crystal sea has a quality similar to coral reef sections found in Queensland's north.

Circular Quay

The Quay is the heart of the Sydney Ferry network. At any given time, at least one of these green-hulled vessels will be visible at the docks, either accepting passengers or waiting for them to disembark. They then make their way slowly to and from the middle harbour on routes that stretch north-east to Manly and west towards Parramatta River.

The City from the Harbour

A passing ferry provides a platform for discovering the pleasant geometry of the CBD, which seems to follow a natural arc across its skyline. The dense cluster of skyscrapers lends Sydney a unique and attractively ordered structure when viewed from middle distance.

The Rocks

The Rocks nestles on the western edge of Circular Quay, the initial point of colonial settlement. Preservation of the area's heritage was the subject of conflict during the 1970s, but eventually common sense prevailed and the region has undergone restoration and improvement to become popular with both locals and tourists. The architecture transports the visitor to a previous era, and even products of modern consumerism attempt to blend in with the nostalgic theme.

Queen Victoria Building

Built in 1898 in the Byzantine style, this historic and beautiful building was restored in the 1980s at a cost exceeding $75 million. Pierre Cardin, obviously impressed with the work, christened it 'the most beautiful shopping centre in the world' on a visit to Sydney. Its exclusive cafes and shops are housed in an exquisite setting lavish enough to match the prices of their merchandise. Stunning architecture, a replica of the Crown Jewels, and various other monuments and displays ensure that a browse through the QVB does not have to involve shopping to be enjoyed.

The City from Darling Harbour
Situated on the the northern end of Cockle Bay is the popular Sydney Aquarium, seen here with its outer edges met by moored boats. Behind it stands the concrete and glass of the middle city, with the golden spire of Sydney Tower shining in the background - its height making it impossible to be obscured within its environment.

Cockle Bay Wharf

Modern, innovative and precise architecture is a feature of the Cockle Bay Wharf development, complemented by the space-age IMAX Theatre hovering at its southern end. During the lunch hour and in the evening, corporate types stream from their multi-window offices to patronise the many cafes, bars and restaurants found along this trendy strip. At night, an influx of people eager to participate in the atmosphere ensures the area bustles with life.

Sydney Skyline at Sunset
In the evening, a disappearing sun projects its fading light through streaks of cloud while the silhouettes of boats and buildings become the forefront of a golden curtain. Sydney Tower, thin and distant, manages to stand majestically above surrounding skyscrapers; an unmistakable icon in the city's centre.

Hyde Park
The impressive Archibald Fountain, with its fanning peacock-pattern spray, captures the attention of people strolling through the northern section of Hyde Park. The western boundary of the park adjoins the hectic commerce-and-trade climate of Market and Elizabeth Streets while St Mary's Cathedral to the east encourages quiet contemplation and prayer.

Centennial Park

Historically significant, Centennial Park commemorates the birthplace of the nation. It was at this site in 1901 that Australia was officially declared a federation of states. In this view from the park, the city skyline several kilometres to the northeast reveals itself above the manicured gardens. Well-tended greenery lines both sides of one of the many narrow roads cutting a swathe through the extensive area.

Town Hall
The design of the Sydney Town Hall draws on the French Renaissance period, and it was built between 1868 and 1889. Located on George Street, its steps are often crammed with people catching their breath, snacking on fast food, making a protest, selling something suspect or busking with limited talent. Its sandstone spires and recesses are aesthetically floodlit at night.

notable buildings

Art Gallery of New South Wales

This spectacular building is home to a vast contemporary collection of Australian, European and Asian Art, and a fine collection of Aboriginal paintings and artifacts. The names of famous artists are set in stone on the front of the building, upon the tier just below the roof. Two statues of mounted horseman grace the patches of lawn on either side of the entrance. In this enriching environment, you can immerse yourself in culture and history before relaxing and absorbing it all among the flora of the Domain across the road or in the Botanical Gardens nearby.

'he War Memorial, Hyde Park

'rotruding from the lush surrounds of Hyde Park, this enormous monument 'ommemorates those who gave their lives during war - a significant proportion of 'he Australian population each time. It was built after the First World War but also 'ymbolises every military sacrifice made since.

The poignant carvings on the Memorial pitch solemn order against the rage of battle, evoking a sense of reflection and an awareness of great loss.

Government House, Botanical Gardens

This astonishing building is the state's finest example of sophisticated Gothic Revival, and it took eight years to build, finally completed in 1845. Although the battlements, turrets and arches present it for all intents and purposes as a castle, defence was not one of the buildings intended functions, and it was instead given over to the adminstration of colonial affairs. Surrounded by scenic gardens in one of the city's finest corners, it now acts as a pleasant welcoming venue for official receptions.

't Mary's Cathedral
)utmatched in its Gothic Revival style only by Government House, St Mary's :athedral is the awesome legacy of a 62-year project completed in 1928. Vaulted :eilings, intricate statues, period-piece gargoyles and crafted side altars make the church interior both beautiful and fascinating. Perhaps the pinnacle of the labour is the outstanding stained glass windows depicting scenes in the life of the Blessed Virgin Mary, and of the early days of the Catholic Church in Australia.

Bondi
On sultry days, such scenes as this are common at Bondi, home of Sydney's most famous beach. Crowds filter through even the farthest reaches of the city to stake their claim to a golden patch of sand for a few hours. Inviting ocean temperatures and the safety provided be an elite surf life-saving team have made this coastal stretch extremely popular during the summer months.

With the quality of Bondi's waves so dependent on wind direction, the type of surf can range from good boarding conditions to little more than a paddle pool. In the event of disappointment there are plenty of cafes and restaurants to attend as well as the famous Bondi Beach Pavillion, built in 1928 and given a recent facelift.
Bondi has its own distinct lifestyle, and the pace slows as soon as you cross into its suburban boundary.

Bronte
Squeezed between Tamarama and Clovelly, Bronte frequently experiences rough surf. It is a popular haven for boarders of all types, as this enthusiast shows. Young, wetsuit-clad men and women perform their daily pilgrimage to the sea in search of rolling waves brought in by Pacific Ocean currents. It is a sight which is certainly not exclusive to Bronte, being replicated on any favourable summer morning or afternoon along metropolitan Sydney's entire coastal length.

Bennett Street, Surry Hills

Terrace housing is a quaint and common feature of inner-suburban dwelling. Density of living in popular regions with close proximity to the city means that town houses, duplexes and apartments are basically the only form of accommodation on offer. Sometimes these linked buildings stretch the distance of a whole street, separated in appearance only by exterior colours and the barest architectural trimmings. Those craving a big backyard head into the outer suburbs while inner-suburbanites tend to their pots on two-square-metre balconies, and choose the lifestyle instead. Although the frontal facade of these places is standard and often unimpressive, the interior is typically where owner's exert their effort, and they are often breathtaking.

Newtown, off King Street

Graffiti is certainly a problem in the inner-city, with every public and private possession not under constant surveillance being open to the possibility of receiving a few expletive strokes from a spray-can-wielding delinquent. However, when plain fading white brick walls are transformed into works of indigenous art, the result is astounding and welcome.

This vibrant mix of traditional Aboringal style with modern verve and flair is a far cry from the vandalising paint that finds its way onto train carriages, abandoned sheds and local fences. It is also a proud leap forward from the Kakadu Rock Art it echoes. The work is located in Newtown - the cultural centre of liberal alternative youths epitomising New Age living.

'he Zoo

'aronga Park Zoo is one of the most scenic in the world. It occupies a prime selection of 'ydney real estate in Mosman, the exclusive suburb north across the harbour from the 'ity centre. Australia's best collection of native and exotic animals are kept here, making the attraction imperative for visitors and continually popular with Sydney residents. Views from within the park are superb, yet this seemingly disinterested giraffe is apparently oblivious to the market-value of his panoramic home.

Echo Point
On the outskirts of Katoomba, at the end of Cliff Drive, Echo Point forms a sheer drop into the valley far below. The unusual rock formations not far from the lookout and impossible to miss are called 'The Three Sisters'. These distinguishable spires jutting towards the sky are located in the Blue Mountains National Park. They are important figures in Aboriginal legend, representing three young sisters in an old story.

he Olympic City

ydney's most recent fame centres on its role as host of the new millenium's first)lympic Games. The events of Sydney 2000 unfold in the last two weeks of eptember, capturing the world's attention. A concentration on modern architecture leading the Zeitgeist of the twentieth century into the next Age - is the definitive element of the Olympic site. Homebush, suitably located in Sydney's geographic centre, is set back from the banks of the Parramatta River. With its domes, arcs and cylindrical shapes, the site seems to spring like a spaceport from science fiction out of its green surrounds.

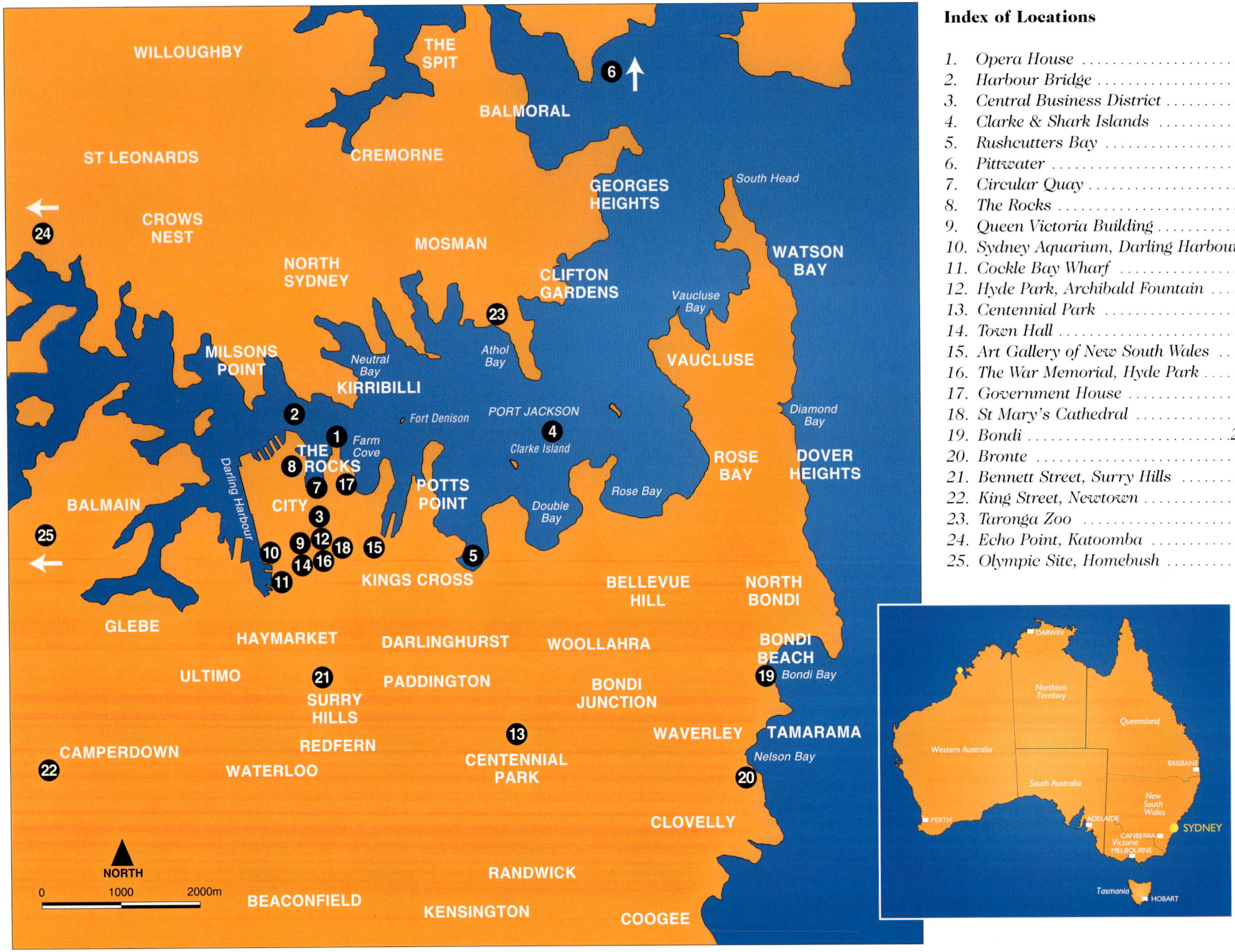

WILLOUGHBY
THE SPIT
BALMORAL
ST LEONARDS
CREMORNE
GEORGES HEIGHTS
South Head
CROWS NEST
MOSMAN
WATSON BAY
NORTH SYDNEY
CLIFTON GARDENS
Vaucluse Bay
MILSONS POINT
Neutral Bay
Athol Bay
VAUCLUSE
KIRRIBILLI
Fort Denison
PORT JACKSON
Diamond Bay
Farm Cove
THE ROCKS
Clarke Island
ROSE BAY
DOVER HEIGHTS
Darling Harbour
POTTS POINT
Rose Bay
BALMAIN
CITY
Double Bay
KINGS CROSS
BELLEVUE HILL
NORTH BONDI
GLEBE
HAYMARKET
DARLINGHURST
WOOLLAHRA
BONDI BEACH
ULTIMO
Bondi Bay
PADDINGTON
BONDI JUNCTION
SURRY HILLS
WAVERLEY
TAMARAMA
CAMPERDOWN
REDFERN
CENTENNIAL PARK
Nelson Bay
WATERLOO
CLOVELLY
NORTH
RANDWICK
0 1000 2000m
BEACONFIELD
KENSINGTON
COOGEE

Index of Locations

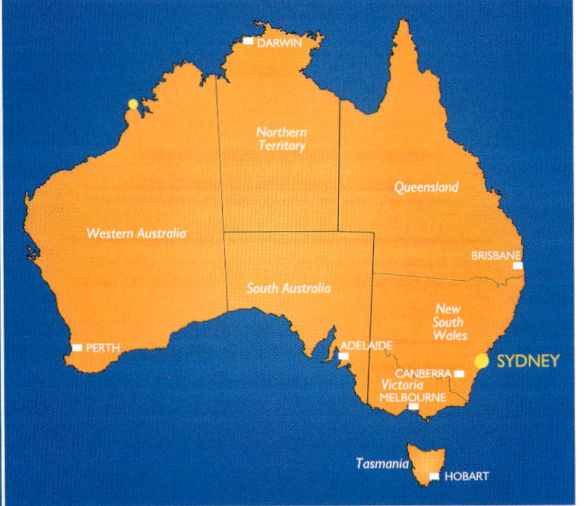